THE WORLD AROUND ME

HELPFUL PEOPLE
IN MY WORLD

Written by
Hermione Redshaw

KidHaven
PUBLISHING

Published in 2023 by **KidHaven Publishing,**
an Imprint of Greenhaven Publishing, LLC
2544 Clinton St., Buffalo, NY 14224

© 2022 Booklife Publishing
This edition is published by arrangement with Booklife Publishing

Written by: Hermione Redshaw
Edited by: William Anthony
Illustrated by: Amy Li

Font (cover, page 1) courtesy of cuppuccino on Shutterstock.com. With thanks to Getty Images, Thinkstock Photo and iStockphoto.

Cataloging-in-Publication Data

Names: Redshaw, Hermione, author. | Li, Amy, illustrator.
Title: Helpful people in my world / by Hermione Redshaw, illustrated by Amy Li.
Description: New York : KidHaven Publishing, 2023. | Series: The world around me
Identifiers: ISBN 9781534543300 (pbk.) | ISBN 9781534543324 (library bound) | ISBN 9781534543331 (ebook)
Subjects: LCSH: Community-based social services--Juvenile literature.| Human services--Juvenile literature.
Classification: LCC HV40.R394 2023 | DDC 361.8--dc23

All rights reserved. No part of this book may be reproduced in any form without permission in writing from the publisher, except by a reviewer.

Manufactured in the United States of America

CPSIA compliance information: Batch #CWKH23
For further information contact Greenhaven Publishing LLC at 1-844-317-7404

Please visit our website, www.greenhavenpublishing.com. For a free color catalog of all our high-quality books, call toll free 1-844-317-7404 or fax 1-844-317-7405.

Find us on

Sofia knows all about **helpful people!**
She sees them every day.

Sofia is waiting for a package.

The postal worker brings Sofia's package to the door.

Sofia is doing her work at school. She is stuck.

At the store, Sofia cannot reach the biscuits.

A shop assistant gets the biscuits for her.

Sofia goes to the dentist. Her teeth are sore.

The dentist helps her.
Sofia's teeth are better now.

Sofia is dancing at ballet class.
She does not know the moves.

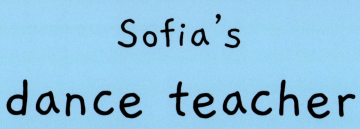

Sofia's dance teacher shows her the moves.

Sofia can dance now.

Sofia visits the doctor.

She feels ill.

The doctor helps her. Sofia feels better now.

A firefighter climbs up the tree.

The cat is safe.

The cat needs to go to the vet.

The vet helps the cat.

The cat is better now.

Sofia wants to be a teacher.